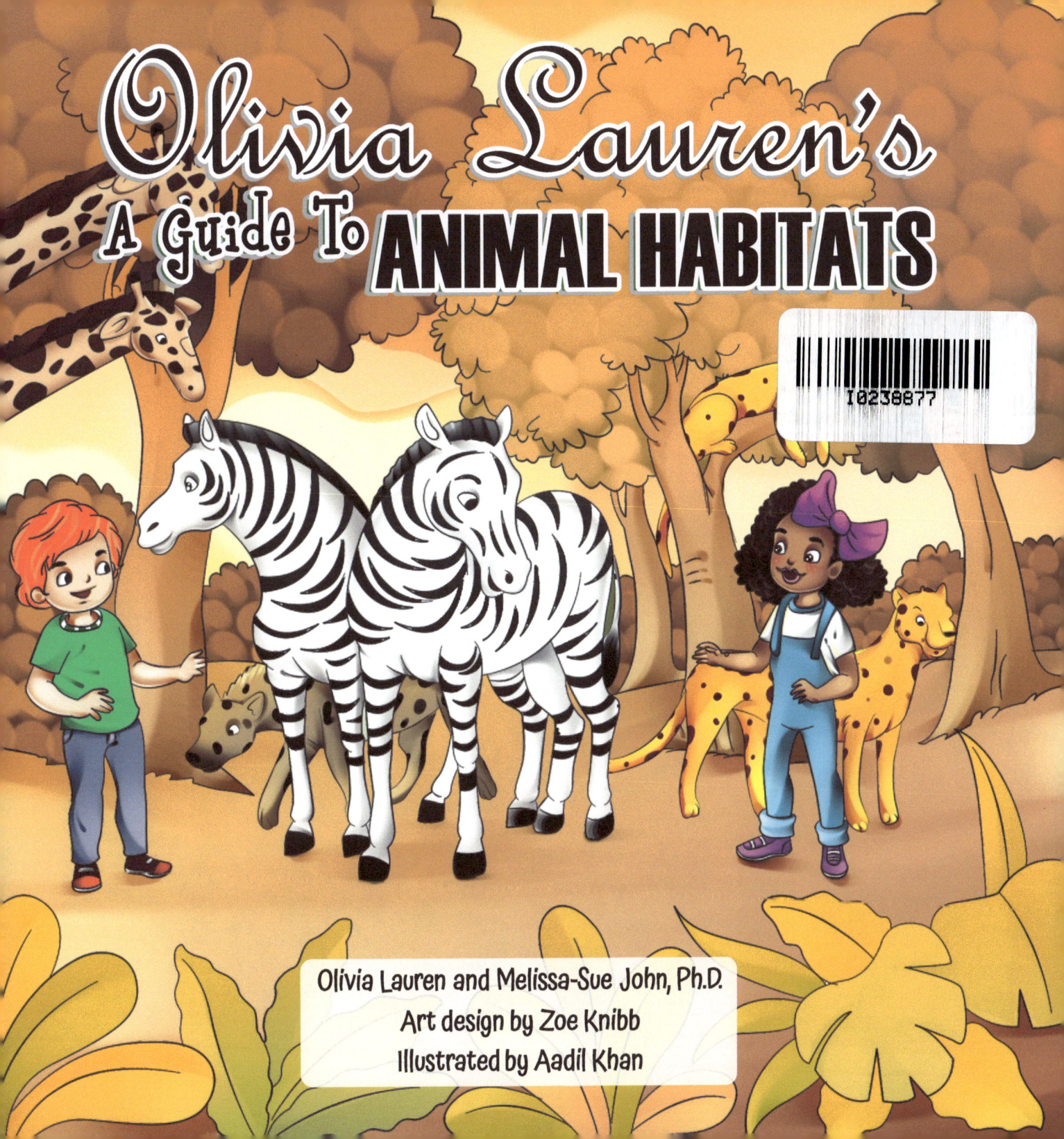

All rights reserved. In accordance with the U.S. Copyright Act of 1976, the scanning, uploading, and electronic sharing of any part of this book without the permission of the publisher constitutes unlawful piracy and theft of the author's intellectual property. If you would like to use material from the book (other than for review purposes), prior written permission must be obtained by contacting the publisher at laurensimonepubs@gmail.com. Thank you for your support of the author's rights.

Library of Congress Cataloging-in-Publication Data
Lauren, Olivia and John, Melissa-Sue
Olivia Lauren's Guide to Animal Habitats
Olivia Lauren
p. cm.
Illustrated by Aadil Khan and Zoe Knibb
Summary: A kid friendly, mixed media, multicultural approach to learning about different types of animal habitats in their various locations. Olivia Lauren travels with several friends to learn about different habitats.
ISBN -13: 978-0997952070
Title I. Series. Olivia Lauren
1. Habitat 2. Biome 3. Climate 4. STEM 5. Geography
2022923713

www.laurensimonepubs.com
laurensimonepubs@gmail.com
@laurensimonepubs

To Matthew John, Rosamond White, Janet Reynolds, Stefanie Sargis, Dr. CaTameron Bobino, Dr. Tamira Butler-Likely, Dr. Robin Walker, and Terese Slater for your valuable feedback and assistance in the creation of this book.

My home keeps me safe from the wind and the rain, the snow and the hail. My home is a refuge from all kinds of weather. Inside we play, we eat, and we do chores together. Looking out on this beautiful sunny day, I watch the birds fly by and squirrels busily gathering their winter supply. I can't help but to wonder how all these animals get by.

How wonderful it would be to gather up my friends for an exploration to learn about animals' habitats in various locations. If Harriet likes, we can first hike through the FOREST listening to the chorus of songbirds, searching for rabbits and watching squirrels like a tourist!

Next, let's go to Brazil to meet my friend, Rosa. She takes us to see the Amazon rainforest, the largest RAINFOREST in the world, where we find fluttering butterflies.

After, we will fly to Canada since it has the largest **TAIGAS.** Snowy or rainy, it's filled with wolves, beavers, hares, and red squirrels.

wolf

beaver

hare

Red squirrel

Located in North Africa is the Sahara **DESERT**, the largest desert in the world. Here we are riding a camel, avoiding poisonous scorpions, and admiring a unique bird.

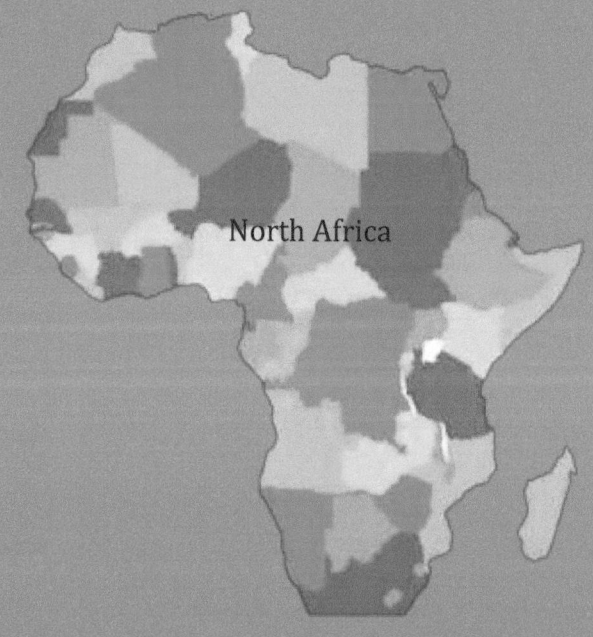
North Africa

While nestled in the south of Africa, we stay at a giraffe manor, then caravan through the **SAVANNA**.

Back in the U.S., Indira and I head into the **GRASSLANDS.** We find grazing bison inhabiting this flat land. Wild horses galloping and migrating birds flying in their aerial grandstand.

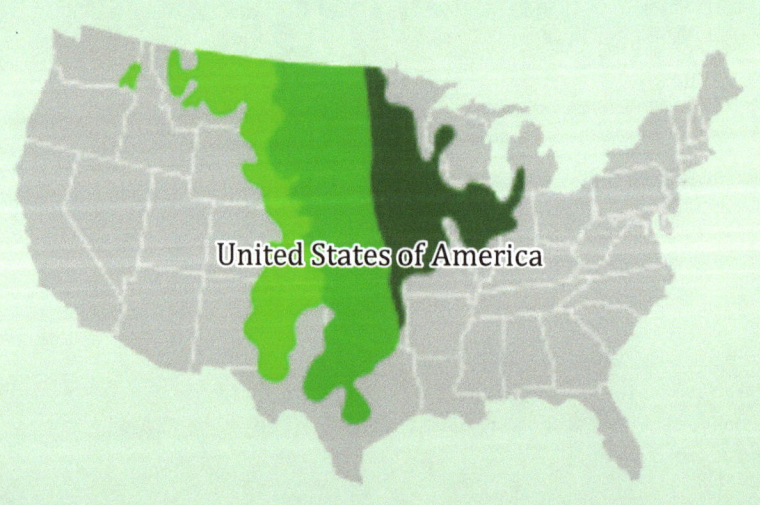

Xavier and I dance our way into New Orleans to muster up a muskrat, mingle with the minks, and wrestle with the alligators in the **SWAMPS** of the bayou.

alligator

mink

muskrat

Vera and I climb up the **MOUNTAIN** hoping to be welcomed in the cold habitats of the goats, deer, and bears.

Taj and I then mosey over to the **POLAR** region of Alaska to parle with the Polar Bears outside of their icy caves.

polar bear

After visiting the cold habitats, Adam and I decide on a warm, tropical destination to educate ourselves on **MARINE** life. We see dancing dolphins, schools of fish, and a beautiful octopus.

dolphin

fish

octopus

Traveling the world to see different animal habitats would be such fun. I love learning with my friends, even if it is just in my imagination!

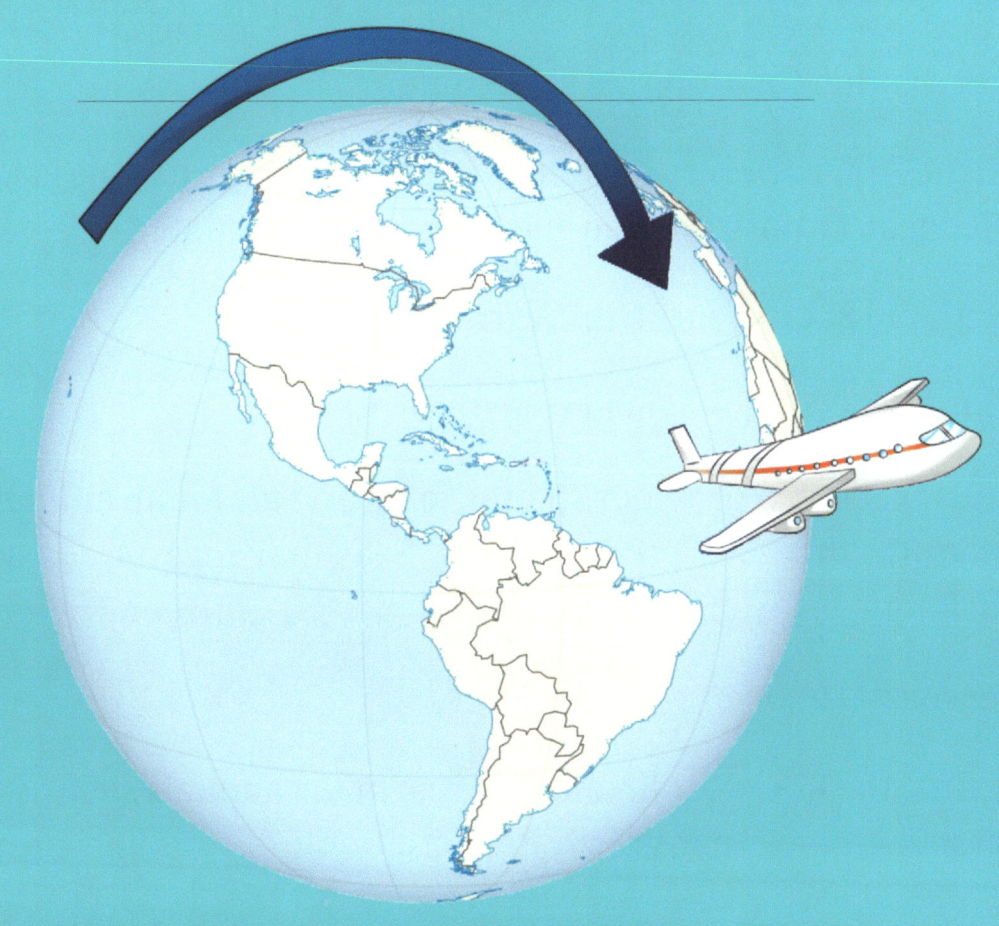

GLOSSARY

Alpine: a mountain region.

Biome: habitats in the same climate. There are five major types of biomes: aquatic, grassland, forest, desert, and tundra, though some of these biomes can be further divided into more specific categories, such as freshwater, marine, savanna, tropical rainforest, temperate rainforest, and taiga.

Boreal forest: another name for taiga habitat.

Climate: weather for a long period of time.

Desert: the Sahara Desert, located in northern Africa. It is the largest desert in the world. It doesn't rain very often and is close to the equator.

Forest: a large habitat with a thick growth of trees.

Grassland: a large habitat made mostly of grass.

Habitat: a place that provides shelter, food, and air for an animal. These habitats are Polar, Tundra, Evergreen forests, Seasonal forests, Grasslands, Deserts, Tropical Rainforests, and Oceans.

Marine: coastal or open ocean habitats.

Mountains: the Rocky Mountains have so many animals such as elk, moose, deer, bighorn sheep, black bear, grizzly bear, gray wolf, coyote, and mountain goats.

Ocean: a type of marine habitat.

Polar: also called a tundra, is the coldest and driest of all the habitats. The tundra is in the North Pole. Because it is so cold, only a few animals are found here.

Rainforest: the rainforest is also called a tropical forest. the largest rainforest is in Brazil.

Savanna: a tropical grassland with lots of shrubs and bushes. The largest savanna is in Africa.

Shelter: a place that provides a home and protection from nature.

Taiga: a forest with many evergreen trees such as pine, fir, spruce, and other cone-bearing trees. The taiga is also called the Boreal forest. The largest taigas are found in Russia and Canada. There are more than 85 species living in the taigas including wolves, beavers, hares, and red squirrels.

Temperate forest: a forest is a large area with many trees, mosses, and flowers. A temperate forest is also called a deciduous forest. Deciduous trees shed leaves during the winter.

Temperate grasslands: are usually found between deserts and forests. They can be found in the United Kingdom, United States, and Canada. I wonder what animals we will discover here. The variety of animals is low, but the number of animals is high. In the U.S., you may find many grazing animals, such as the bison or the pronghorn.

Wetlands: peatlands of Siberia, the Mangrove swamps in Florida, or the bayous of Louisiana. Swamps, peatlands, and bayous are types of wetlands.

ART ACTIVITY
Draw and color your favorite habitat.

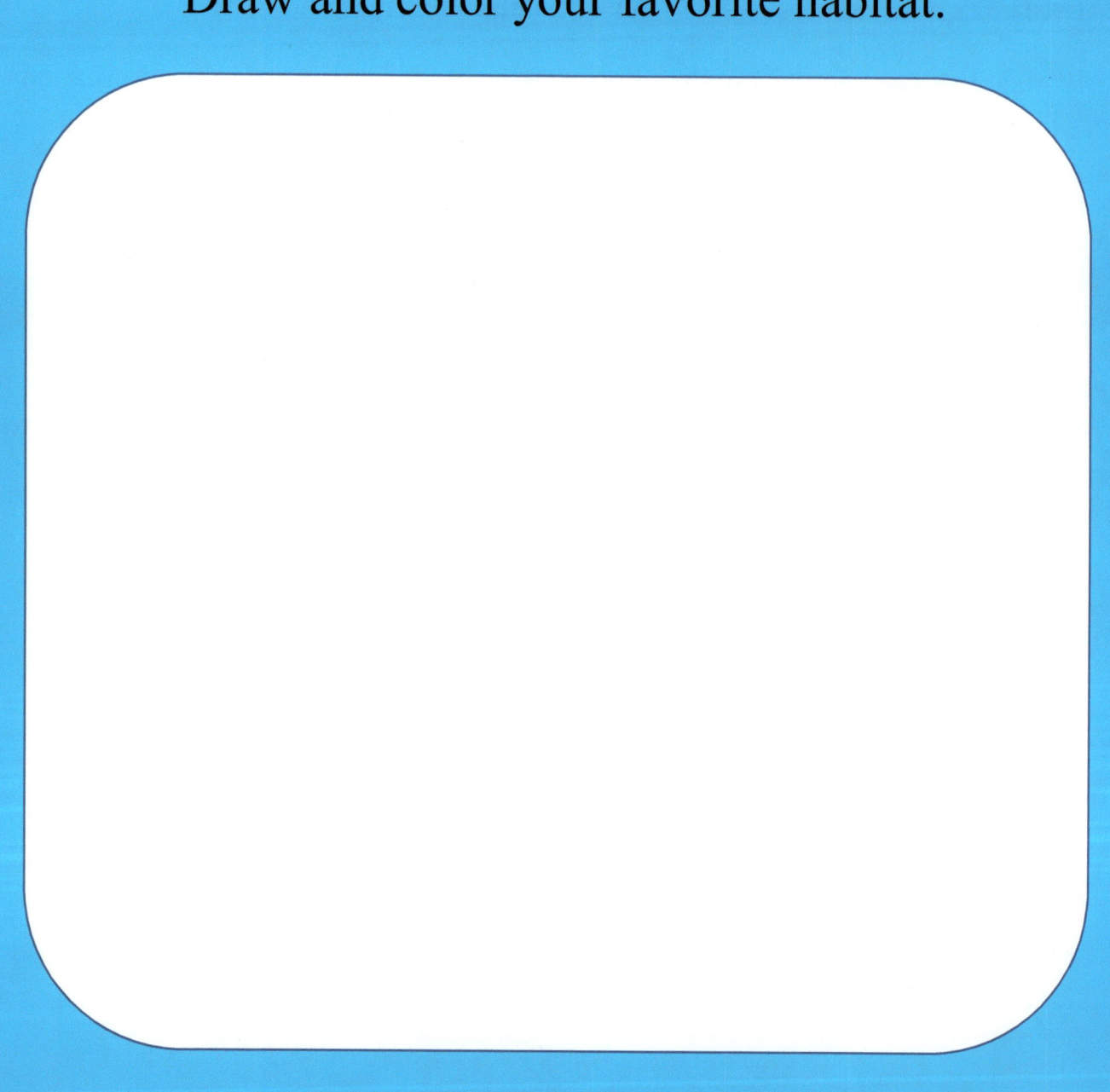

COMPREHENSION ACTIVITY

Name two cold habitats.

Name two wet habitats.

Name two dry habitats.

Name three habitats with trees.

What is the largest habitat?

What is another name for the polar region?

What is another name for savanna?

SCIENCE ACTIVITY

Match the animal with the correct habitat.

 Temperate Forest

 Rain forest

Taiga

 Desert

Grasslands

 Savanna

Wetlands

 Mountains

Tundra

 Ocean

ABOUT THE AUTHORS

Olivia Lauren was born November 5, 2007, in Farmington, CT. She enjoys painting, acting, reading, and writing. She is an intelligent and hardworking student. Olivia Lauren has been featured in commercials, TV shows, films, music videos ("Polaridad" by Alex Ferreira, "My Daughter's Living Room" by Alge, and "StereoTypes" by Black Violin), theater productions, and print media *(Big City Kids, Wild Child, AI Magazine, Writer's Magazine, KidLit Magazine, The Bubblah, Kidlio,* and the Hartford Courant). Follow Olivia Lauren on Instagram and Facebook: @olivialaurenj

Dr. Melissa-Sue John is a wife, the mother of Alyssa Simone and Olivia Lauren, an author, publisher, psychology professor, and researcher. She is proud of her Jamaican heritage and to be a graduate of Harrison's Preparatory School and Holy Childhood High School. After high school, she moved to the U.S. where she earned her Bachelor of Arts degree from Hunter College, CUNY and masters and doctoral degrees from the University of Connecticut. She enjoys lecturing and mentoring students. These various roles led her to write children's literature with her two daughters and she now serves as the Chief Executive Operator and Blogger of Lauren Simone Publishing House. Please write us a review, visit our blog, and follow on Instagram: @laurensimonepubs.

ABOUT THE ILLUSTRATORS

Zoe is an 11-year-old actress, model, and artist who resides in New York. Zoe has worked with companies like Nickelodeon, Sprout, Best Buy, and Walmart. In her spare time, she enjoys drawing and painting. Zoe joined Lauren Simone Publishing House in 2020 where she began to illustrate the 6th book in the Olivia Lauren series. She also enjoys making bar soaps and dancing. Zoe is currently in the 6th grade, has maintained Honor Roll and continues to excel academically. Zoe is involved in extracurricular activities including Lego robotics and is on her school's robotics team. She is also involved in the Student Council and serves as a Model United Nation's representative. Zoe's aspiration is to become a Pediatrician, but she is considering a dual major in Graphic Arts and Pre-Med. Follow her journey on Instagram: @Zoesimone41

Aadil Khan was born in Meerut, India, and lives in Delhi, India. He is an experienced graphic designer with a love for illustrating children's books. He owns his own company (Kidillus), where he uses the latest trends in illustration. He provides a complete service from designing covers and illustrations to layout design and typesetting. When he is not working, he is spending time with family, traveling, or enjoying sports, specifically racing.